Ninja Dual Zone Air Fryer Cookbook

Easy, Foolproof Recipes

for Your Air Fryer

Sandra Howarth

© **Copyright 2021 Sandra Howarth - All Rights Reserved.**

In no way is it legal to reproduce, duplicate, or transmit any part of this document by either electronic means or in printed format. Recording of this publication is strictly prohibited, and any storage of this material is not allowed unless with written permission from the publisher. All rights reserved.

The information provided herein is stated to be truthful and consistent, in that any liability, regarding inattention or otherwise, by any usage or abuse of any policies, processes, or directions contained within is the solitary and complete responsibility of the recipient reader. Under no circumstances will any legal liability or blame be held against the publisher for any reparation, damages, or monetary loss due to the information herein, either directly or indirectly.

Respective authors own all copyrights not held by the publisher.

Legal Notice:

This book is copyright protected. This is only for personal use. You cannot amend, distribute, sell, use, quote or paraphrase any part of the content within this book without the consent of the author or copyright owner. Legal action will be pursued if this is breached.

Disclaimer Notice:

Please note the information contained within this document is for educational and entertainment purposes only. Every attempt has been made to provide accurate, up-to-date and reliable, complete information. No warranties of any kind are expressed or implied. Readers acknowledge that the author is not engaging in the rendering of legal, financial, medical or professional advice.

By reading this document, the reader agrees that under no circumstances are we responsible for any losses, direct or indirect, which are incurred as a result of the use of information contained within this document, including, but not limited to, errors, omissions, or inaccuracies.

CONTENTS

AIR FRYING BASICS..6

    Health Benefits..6

BREAKFAST AND BRUNCH RECIPES..8

    Potato Rosti..8

    Eggs In Bread Cups...9

    Sweet Potato Tots..10

    Egg & Spinach Tart...11

    Roasted Cauliflower..12

    Breakfast Frittata..13

    Cinnamon And Sugar Doughnuts..14

    Spinach & Tomato Frittata..15

    Bacon & Spinach Muffins..16

    Cinnamon French Toasts..17

    Tomato Quiche..18

    Sausage With Eggs & Avocado..19

    Bell Pepper Omelet...20

    Tex-mex Hash Browns...21

    Eggs In Avocado Cups...22

SNACK & DESSERT RECIPES..23

    Air Fryer Beignets..23

    Sugar And Cinnamon Doughnuts..24

    Honeyed Banana...25

    Red Velvet Cupcakes..26

    Chocolate Cake...27

    Jalapeño Poppers..28

Spicy Spinach Chips 29

Fried Pickles 30

Air-fried Butter Cake 31

Buffalo Chicken Wings 32

MEAT RECIPES 33

Beef Kabobs 33

Beef Sirloin Roast 34

Herbed Pork Chops 35

Glazed Lamb Chops 36

Italian-style Meatballs 37

Braised Lamb Shanks 38

Lamb Sirloin Steak 39

Pork Meatloaf 40

Ranch Pork Chops 41

Stuffed Pork Roll 42

POULTRY RECIPES 43

Herbed & Spiced Turkey Breast 43

Herbed Chicken Drumsticks 44

Blackened Chicken Breast 45

Seasoned Chicken Tenders 46

Egg Frittata 47

Olive-brined Turkey Breast 48

Air Fryer Chicken Wings 49

Spiced Chicken Thighs 50

Nashville Chicken 51

Roasted Cornish Game Hen 52

Asian Deviled Eggs 53

Crispy Roasted Chicken 54

Turkish Chicken Kebab 55

Bang-bang Chicken..56

Peruvian Chicken Drumsticks & Green Crema..57

FISH & SEAFOOD RECIPES..58

Lemon Dill Mahi Mahi...58

Crumbed Fish..59

Spiced Tilapia..60

Lemony Shrimp..61

Crusted Salmon..62

Herbed Salmon..63

Seasoned Catfish...64

Halibut & Shrimp with Pasta..65

Crusted Sole...66

Glazed Salmon...67

VEGETARIAN AND VEGAN RECIPES..68

Glazed Mushrooms...68

Tofu With Broccoli...69

Fried Chickpeas...70

Roasted Okra...71

Roasted Vegetables..72

Potato-skin Wedges..73

Broccoli With Cauliflower...74

Buttered Veggies...75

Basil Tomatoes..76

Sweet & Tangy Mushrooms..77

Potato Gratin...78

Cheesy Kale...79

Parmesan Asparagus...80

Green Beans & Mushroom Casserole...81

Spicy Potato..82

AIR FRYING BASICS

In the simplest of terms, an air-fryer is a compact cylindrical countertop convection oven. It's a kitchen appliance that uses superheated air to cook foods, giving results very similar to deep-frying or high-temperature roasting. Many of us have convection ovens in our kitchens. In a standard oven, air is heated and the hot air cooks the food. In a convection oven, air is heated and then blown around by a fan. This creates more energy and consequently cooks foods faster and more evenly.

Air fryers use the same technology as convection ovens, but instead of blowing the air around a large rectangular box, it is blown around in a compact cylinder and the food sits in a perforated basket. This is much more efficient and creates an intense environment of heat from which the food cannot escape. The result is food with a crispy brown exterior and moist tender interior – results similar to deep-frying, but without all the oil and fat needed to deep-fry. In fact, when you are air-frying, you usually use no more than one tbsp. of oil!

Better still, an air fryer doesn't just cook foods that you would usually deep-fry. It can cook any foods that you would normally cook in your oven or microwave as well. It is a great tool for re-heating foods without making them rubbery, and is a perfect and quick way to prepare ingredients as well as make meals. To me, it is the best new kitchen appliance that has been introduced in recent years.

Health Benefits

Obviously, because it can produce results similar to deep-frying using a tiny fraction of the oil needed to deep-fry, the health benefits are apparent. When deep-frying, you submerge the food in oil and oil is inevitably absorbed by the food. In an air fryer, you still use oil because oil is what helps crisp and brown many foods, but you really don't need more than one tbsp. at a time. Instead of putting the tbsp. of oil in the air fryer, you simply toss foods with oil and then place them in the air fryer basket. In fact, spraying the foods lightly with oil is an even easier way to get foods evenly coated with the least amount of oil. Investing in a kitchen spray bottle is a great idea if you have an air fryer.

QUICK AND ENERGY EFFICIENT

We all know that sometimes it can take fifteen to twenty minutes to pre-heat our standard ovens. Because the air fryer is so compact, that pre-heat time is cut down to two or three minutes! That's a huge savings in time as well as energy. In the summer, you can pre-heat your air fryer and not heat up the whole kitchen. In addition, the intense heat created in the air fryer cooks foods quickly, about 20% faster than in an oven, so you're saving time and energy there as well. No one these days seems to have time to spare, so this should please everyone!

SAFE AND EASY TO USE

Air-frying is safer and easier than deep-frying. Most air fryers have settings for time and temperature. You simply enter both and press start. It doesn't get much easier than that! When deep-frying, you have to heat a large pot of oil on the stovetop, use a deep-frying thermometer to register the temperature and then monitor the heat below the pot to maintain that temperature. On top of it all, you are dealing with a lot of oil, which can be heavy to move, dangerous if it gets too hot, and is cumbersome and annoying to drain and dispose of. Why bother if you can get the same results so much more easily with an air fryer?

CLEAN AND TIDY

I didn't earn the "Miss Tidy Bed" badge in brownies for no reason! I love keeping the kitchen clean and tidy when I'm cooking and after I've been cooking. The air fryer fits into my world perfectly. It cooks foods in a contained space and that keeps the food from splattering anywhere. Period. You can even cook bacon in the air fryer without making a mess (do remember the tip to put a little water in the drawer below to prevent the bacon grease from smoking). It is simple and straightforward to clean and keep clean, and you know what they say about cleanliness...

USING AIR FRYERS TO PREPARE INGREDIENTS

So often, I find myself turning to the air fryer to cook ingredients for meals that might not even call for an air fryer. Don't underestimate the convenience of quickly toasting some nuts for a salad, or roasting a pepper for pasta, or quickly cooking bacon for an egg sandwich. Ingredients in recipes often come with a qualifier – "walnuts, toasted", or "bread cubes, toasted" – and the air fryer comes to the rescue, once again saving precious time.

Breakfast And Brunch Recipes
Potato Rosti

Servings: 2
Cooking Time: 15 Mins

Ingredients:
- ½ lb. potatoes, peeled, grated and squeezed
- ½ tbsp. fresh rosemary, chopped finely
- ½ tbsp. fresh thyme, chopped finely
- 1/8 tsp. red pepper flakes, crushed
- Salt and ground black pepper, as required
- 2 tbsp. butter, softened

Directions:
1. In a bowl, mix together the potato, herbs, red pepper flakes, salt and black pepper.
2. Press "Power Button" of Ninja Foodi Digital Air Fry Oven and turn the dial to select the "Air Fry" mode.
3. Press the Time button and again turn the dial to set the cooking time to 15 minutes.
4. Now push the Temp button and rotate the dial to set the temperature at 355 degrees F.
5. Press "Start/Pause" button to start.
6. When the unit beeps to show that it is preheated, open the lid and lightly, grease the sheet pan.
7. Arrange the potato mixture into the "Sheet Pan" and shape it into an even circle.
8. Insert the "Sheet Pan" in the oven.
9. Cut the potato rosti into wedges.
10. Top with the butter and serve immediately.

Eggs In Bread Cups

Servings: 4
Cooking Time: 23 Mins

Ingredients:
- 4 bacon slices
- 2 bread slices, crust removed
- 4 eggs
- Salt and freshly ground black pepper, to taste

Directions:
1. Grease 4 C. of a muffin tin and set aside.
2. Heat a small frying pan over medium-high heat and cook the bacon slices for about 2-3 minutes.
3. With a slotted spoon, transfer the bacon slice onto a paper towel-lined plate to cool.
4. Break each bread slice in half.
5. Arrange 1 bread slices half in each of the prepared muffin C. and press slightly.
6. Now, arrange 1 bacon slice over each bread slice in a circular shape.
7. Crack 1 egg into each muffin C. and sprinkle with salt and black pepper.
8. Press "Power Button" of Ninja Foodi Digital Air Fry Oven and turn the dial to select "Air Bake" mode.
9. Press "Time Button" and again turn the dial to set the cooking time to 20 minutes.
10. Now push "Temp Button" and rotate the dial to set the temperature at 350 degrees F.
11. Press "Start/Pause" button to start.
12. When the unit beeps to show that it is preheated, open the lid.
13. Arrange the muffin tin over the wire rack and insert in the oven.
14. When cooking time is complete, open the lid and place the muffin tin onto a wire rack for about 10 minutes.
15. Serve warm.
16. Serving Suggestions: Feel free to top the bread C. with fresh herbs of your choice before serving.
17. Variation Tip: Pancetta can be used instead of bacon.

Sweet Potato Tots

Servings: 4
Cooking Time: 1 Hour

Ingredients:
- 1 tbsp. of potato starch
- 2 small sweet potatoes, peeled
- 1-1/4 tsp. kosher salt
- 1/8 tsp. of garlic powder
- ¾ C. ketchup

Directions:
1. Boil water in a medium-sized pot over high heat.
2. Add the potatoes. Cook till it becomes tender. Transfer them to a plate for cooling. Grate them in a mid-sized bowl.
3. Toss gently with garlic powder, 1 tsp. of salt, and potato starch.
4. Shape the mix into tot-shaped cylinders.
5. Apply cooking spray on the air fryer basket.
6. Place half of the tots in a later in your basket. Apply some cooking spray.
7. Cook till it becomes light brown at 400°F.
8. Take out from the frying basket. Sprinkle some salt.
9. Serve with ketchup immediately.

Egg & Spinach Tart

Servings: 4
Cooking Time: 25 Mins

Ingredients:
- 1 puff pastry sheet, trimmed into a 9x13-inch rectangle
- 4 eggs
- ½ C. cheddar cheese, grated
- 7 cooked thick-cut bacon strips
- ½ C. cooked spinach
- 1 egg, lightly beaten

Directions:
1. Arrange the pastry in a lightly greased "Sheet Pan".
2. With a small knife gently, cut a 1-inch border around the edges of the puff pastry without cutting all the way through.
3. With a fork, pierce the center of pastry a few times.
4. Press "Power Button" of Ninja Foodi Digital Air Fry Oven and turn the dial to select the "Air Bake" mode.
5. Press the Time button and again turn the dial to set the cooking time to 10 minutes.
6. Now push the Temp button and rotate the dial to set the temperature at 400 degrees F.
7. Press "Start/Pause" button to start.
8. When the unit beeps to show that it is preheated, open the lid.
9. Insert the "Sheet Pan" in the oven.
10. Remove the "Sheet Pan" from oven and sprinkle the cheese over the center.
11. Place the spinach and bacon in an even layer across the tart.
12. Now, crack the eggs, leaving space between each one.
13. Press "Power Button" of Ninja Foodi Digital Air Fry Oven and turn the dial to select the "Air Bake" mode.
14. Press the Time button and again turn the dial to set the cooking time to 15 minutes.
15. Now push the Temp button and rotate the dial to set the temperature at 400 degrees F.
16. Press "Start/Pause" button to start.
17. When the unit beeps to show that it is preheated, open the lid.
18. Insert the "Sheet Pan" in the oven.
19. Remove the "Sheet Pan" from oven and set aside to cool for 2-3 minutes before cutting.
20. With a pizza cutter, cut into 4 portions and serve.

Roasted Cauliflower

Servings: 2

Cooking Time: 15 Mins

Ingredients:

- 4 C. of cauliflower florets
- 1 tbsp. peanut oil
- 3 cloves garlic
- ½ tsp. smoked paprika
- ½ tsp. of salt

Directions:

1. Preheat your air fryer to 200 degrees C or 400 degrees F.
2. Now cut the garlic into half. Use a knife to smash it.
3. Keep in a bowl with salt, paprika, and oil.
4. Add the cauliflower. Coat well.
5. Transfer the coated cauliflower to your air fryer.
6. Cook for 10 minutes. Shake after 5 minutes.

Breakfast Frittata

Servings: 2
Cooking Time: 20 Mins

Ingredients:
- 4 eggs, beaten lightly
- 4 oz. sausages, cooked and crumbled
- 1 onion, chopped
- 2 tbsp. of red bell pepper, diced
- ½ C. shredded Cheddar cheese

Directions:
1. Bring together the cheese, eggs, sausage, onion, and bell pepper in a bowl.
2. Mix well.
3. Preheat your air fryer to 180 degrees C or 360 degrees F.
4. Apply cooking spray lightly.
5. Keep your egg mix in a prepared cake pan.
6. Now cook in your air fryer till the frittata has become set.

Cinnamon And Sugar Doughnuts

Servings: 9

Cooking Time: 16 Mins

Ingredients:

- 1 tsp. cinnamon
- 1/3 C. of white sugar
- 2 large egg yolks
- 2-1/2 tbsp. of butter, room temperature
- 1-1/2 tsp. baking powder
- 2-1/4 C. of all-purpose flour

Directions:

1. Take a bowl and press your butter and white sugar together in it.
2. Add the egg yolks. Stir till it combines well.
3. Now sift the baking powder, flour, and salt in another bowl.
4. Keep one-third of the flour mix and half of the sour cream into your egg-sugar mixture. Stir till it combines well.
5. Now mix the remaining sour cream and flour. Refrigerate till you can use it.
6. Bring together the cinnamon and one-third sugar in your bowl.
7. Roll half-inch-thick dough.
8. Cut large slices (9) in this dough. Create a small circle in the center. This will make doughnut shapes.
9. Preheat your fryer to 175 degrees C or 350 degrees F.
10. Brush melted butter on both sides of your doughnut.
11. Keep half of the doughnuts in the air fryer's basket.
12. Apply the remaining butter on the cooked doughnuts.
13. Dip into the sugar-cinnamon mix immediately.

Spinach & Tomato Frittata

Servings: 6
Cooking Time: 30 Mins

Ingredients:
- 10 large eggs
- Salt and freshly ground black pepper, to taste
- 1 (5-ounce) bag baby spinach
- 2 C. grape tomatoes, halved
- 4 scallions, sliced thinly
- 8 oz. feta cheese, crumbled
- 3 tbsp. hot olive oil

Directions:
1. In a bowl, place the eggs, salt and black pepper and beat well.
2. Add the spinach, tomatoes, scallions and feta cheese and gently stir to combine.
3. Spread the oil in a baking pan and top with the spinach mixture.
4. Press "Power Button" of Ninja Foodi Digital Air Fry Oven and turn the dial to select "Air Bake" mode.
5. Press "Time Button" and again turn the dial to set the cooking time to 30 minutes.
6. Now push "Temp Button" and rotate the dial to set the temperature at 350 degrees F.
7. Press "Start/Pause" button to start.
8. When the unit beeps to show that it is preheated, open the lid.
9. Arrange pan over the wire rack and insert in the oven.
10. When cooking time is complete, open the lid and place the pan aside for about 5 minutes.
11. Cut into equal-sized wedges and serve hot.
12. Serving Suggestions: Enjoy your frittata with garlicky potatoes.
13. Variation Tip: Pick the right cheese for frittata.

Bacon & Spinach Muffins

Servings: 6
Cooking Time: 17 Mins

Ingredients:

- 6 eggs
- ½ C. milk
- Salt and freshly ground black pepper, to taste
- 1 C. fresh spinach, chopped
- 4 cooked bacon slices, crumbled

Directions:

1. In a bowl, add the eggs, milk, salt and black pepper and beat until well combined.
2. Add the spinach and stir to combine.
3. Divide the spinach mixture into 6 greased C. of an egg bite mold evenly.
4. Press "Power Button" of Ninja Foodi Digital Air Fry Oven and turn the dial to select "Air Fry" mode.
5. Press "Time Button" and again turn the dial to set the cooking time to 17 minutes.
6. Now push "Temp Button" and rotate the dial to set the temperature at 325 degrees F.
7. Press "Start/Pause" button to start.
8. When the unit beeps to show that it is preheated, open the lid.
9. Arrange the mold over the wire rack and insert in the oven.
10. When cooking time is complete, open the lid and place the mold onto a wire rack to cool for about 5 minutes.
11. Top with bacon pieces and serve warm.
12. Serving Suggestions: Serve these muffins with the drizzling of melted butter.
13. Variation Tip: Don't forget to grease the egg bite molds before pacing the egg mixture in them.

Cinnamon French Toasts

Servings: 2
Cooking Time: 5 Mins

Ingredients:
- 2 eggs
- ¼ C. whole milk
- 3 tbsp. sugar
- 2 tsp. olive oil
- 1/8 tsp. vanilla extract
- 1/8 tsp. ground cinnamon
- 4 bread slices

Directions:
1. In a large bowl, add all the ingredients except for bread slices and mix well.
2. Coat the bread slices with egg mixture evenly.
3. Press "Power Button" of Ninja Foodi Digital Air Fry Oven and turn the dial to select "Air Fry" mode.
4. Press "Time Button" and again turn the dial to set the cooking time to 6 minutes.
5. Now push "Temp Button" and rotate the dial to set the temperature at 390 degrees F.
6. Press "Start/Pause" button to start.
7. When the unit beeps to show that it is preheated, open the lid and lightly grease the sheet pan.
8. Arrange the bread slices into the air fry basket and insert in the oven.
9. Flip the bread slices once halfway through.
10. When cooking time is complete, open the lid and transfer the French toast onto serving plates.
11. Serve warm.
12. Serving Suggestions: You can enjoy these French toast with the drizzling of maple syrup.
13. Variation Tip: For best result, soak the bread slices in egg mixture until each slice is thoroughly saturated.

Tomato Quiche

Servings: 2
Cooking Time: 30 Mins

Ingredients:

- 4 eggs
- ¼ C. onion, chopped
- ½ C. tomatoes, chopped
- ½ C. milk
- 1 C. Gouda cheese, shredded
- Salt, to taste

Directions:

1. In a small baking pan, add all the ingredients and mix well.
2. Press "Power Button" of Ninja Foodi Digital Air Fry Oven and turn the dial to select "Air Fry" mode.
3. Press "Time Button" and again turn the dial to set the cooking time to 30 minutes.
4. Now push "Temp Button" and rotate the dial to set the temperature at 340 degrees F.
5. Press "Start/Pause" button to start.
6. When the unit beeps to show that it is preheated, open the lid.
7. Arrange the pan over the wire rack and insert in the oven.
8. When cooking time is complete, open the lid and place the pan aside for about 5 minutes.
9. Cut into equal-sized wedges and serve.
10. Serving Suggestions: Fresh baby spring mix will be a great companion for this quiche.
11. Variation Tip: You can use any kind of fresh veggies for the filling of quiche.

Sausage With Eggs & Avocado

Servings: 2
Cooking Time: 10 Mins

Ingredients:
- 1 tbsp. maple syrup
- 1 tbsp. balsamic vinegar
- 4 cooked chicken sausages
- 2 hard-boiled eggs, peeled
- 1 small avocado, peeled, pitted and sliced

Directions:
1. In a bowl, mix together the maple syrup and vinegar.
2. Coat the sausages with vinegar mixture.
3. Line the "Sheet Pan" with a lightly, grease piece of foil.
4. Arrange the sausages into the prepared "Sheet Pan".
5. Press "Power Button" of Ninja Foodi Digital Air Fry Oven and turn the dial to select the "Air Roast" mode.
6. Press the Time button and again turn the dial to set the cooking time to 10 minutes.
7. Now push the Temp button and rotate the dial to set the temperature at 450 degrees F.
8. Press "Start/Pause" button to start.
9. When the unit beeps to show that it is preheated, open the lid and insert "Sheet Pan" in the oven.
10. Flip the sausages and coat with the remaining syrup mixture once halfway through.
11. Divide the sausages, eggs and avocado slices onto serving plates and serve.

Bell Pepper Omelet

Servings: 2
Cooking Time: 10 Mins

Ingredients:

- 1 tsp. butter
- 1 small onion, sliced
- ½ of green bell pepper, seeded and chopped
- 4 eggs
- ¼ tsp. milk
- Salt and ground black pepper, as required
- ¼ C. Cheddar cheese, grated

Directions:

1. In a skillet, melt the butter over medium heat and cook the onion and bell pepper for about 4-5 minutes.
2. Remove the skillet from heat and set aside to cool slightly.
3. Meanwhile, in a bowl, add the eggs, milk, salt and black pepper and beat well.
4. Add the cooked onion mixture and gently, stir to combine.
5. Place the zucchini mixture into a small baking pan.
6. Press "Power Button" of Ninja Foodi Digital Air Fry Oven and turn the dial to select the "Air Fry" mode.
7. Press the Time button and again turn the dial to set the cooking time to 5 minutes.
8. Now push the Temp button and rotate the dial to set the temperature at 355 degrees F.
9. Press "Start/Pause" button to start.
10. When the unit beeps to show that it is preheated, open the lid.
11. Arrange pan over the "Wire Rack" and insert in the oven.
12. Cut the omelet into 2 portions and serve hot.

Tex-mex Hash Browns

Servings: 4
Cooking Time: 30 Mins

Ingredients:
- 1-1/2 24 oz. potatoes, cut and peeled
- 1 onion, cut into small pieces
- 1 tbsp. of olive oil
- 1 jalapeno, seeded and cut
- 1 red bell pepper, seeded and cut

Directions:
1. Soak the potatoes in water.
2. Preheat your air fryer to 160 degrees C or 320 degrees F.
3. Drain and dry the potatoes using a clean towel.
4. Keep in a bowl.
5. Drizzle some olive oil over the potatoes, coat well.
6. Transfer to the air frying basket.
7. Add the onion, jalapeno, and bell pepper in the bowl.
8. Sprinkle half tsp. olive oil, pepper, and salt. Coat well by tossing.
9. Now transfer your potatoes to the bowl with the veg mix from your fryer.
10. Place the empty basket into the air fryer. Raise the temperature to 180 degrees C or 356 degrees F.
11. Toss the contents of your bowl for mixing the potatoes with the vegetables evenly.
12. Transfer mix into the basket.
13. Cook until the potatoes have become crispy and brown.

Eggs In Avocado Cups

Servings: 2
Cooking Time: 10 Mins

Ingredients:

- 1 avocado, halved and pitted
- 2 large eggs
- Salt and freshly ground black pepper, to taste
- 2 cooked bacon slices, crumbled

Directions:

1. Carefully scoop out about 2 tsp. of flesh from each avocado half.
2. Crack 1 egg in each avocado half and sprinkle with salt and black pepper lightly.
3. Arrange avocado halves onto the greased piece of foil-lined sheet pan.
4. Press "Power Button" of Ninja Foodi Digital Air Fry Oven and turn the dial to select "Air Roast" mode.
5. Press "Time Button" and again turn the dial to set the cooking time to 10 minutes.
6. Now push "Temp Button" and rotate the dial to set the temperature at 375 degrees F.
7. Press "Start/Pause" button to start.
8. When the unit beeps to show that it is preheated, open the lid and insert the sheet pan in the oven.
9. When cooking time is complete, open the lid and transfer the avocado halves onto serving plates.
10. Top each avocado half with bacon pieces and serve.
11. Serving Suggestions: Serve these avocado halves with cherry tomatoes and fresh spinach.
12. Variation Tip: Smoked salmon can be replaced with bacon too.

Snack & Dessert Recipes

Air Fryer Beignets

Servings: 7
Cooking Time: 15 Mins

Ingredients:

- ½ C. all-purpose flour
- 1 egg, separated
- ½ tsp. of baking powder
- 1-1/2 tsp. melted butter
- ¼ C. white sugar
- ½ tsp. of vanilla extract

Directions:

1. Preheat your air fryer to 185 degrees C or 370 degrees F.
2. Whisk together the sugar, flour, butter, egg yolk, vanilla extract, baking powder, salt, and water in a bowl. Combine well by stirring.
3. Use an electric hand mixer to beat the white portion of the egg in a bowl.
4. Fold this into the batter.
5. Now use a small ice cream scoop to add the mold.
6. Keep the mold into the air fryer basket.
7. Fry for 10 minutes in your air fryer.
8. Take out the mold and the pop beignets carefully.
9. Flip them over on a round of parchment paper.
10. Now transfer the parchment round with the beignets into the fryer basket.
11. Cook for 4 more minutes.

Sugar And Cinnamon Doughnuts

Servings: 9
Cooking Time: 16 Mins

Ingredients:

- 2 egg yolks
- 1-1/2 tsp. baking powder
- 2-1/4 C. of all-purpose flour
- 2 tbsp. of butter
- ½ C. of white sugar
- ½ C. sour cream

Directions:

1. Press butter and ½ C. of white sugar together in a bowl. It should get crumbly.
2. Add the egg yolks. Stir to combine well.
3. Now sift baking powder, flour, and salt into another bowl.
4. Place a third of the flour mix and half sour cream into your egg-sugar mix.
5. Combine well by stirring.
6. Mix the remaining sour cream and flour in.
7. Refrigerate this dough until you can use it.
8. Now mix 1/3rd C. of sugar.
9. Roll your dough to half-inch thickness on a work surface.
10. Cut the dough into 9 circles. Create a small circle at the center of each circle. The shape should be like a doughnut.
11. Preheat your air fryer to 175 degrees C or 350 degrees F.
12. Brush half of the melted butter on both sides of your doughnut.
13. Transfer half of the doughnuts into your air fryer basket.
14. Cook for 6 minutes. Apply melted butter on the doughnuts.

Honeyed Banana

Servings: 2
Cooking Time: 10 Mins

Ingredients:
- 1 ripe banana, peeled and sliced lengthwise
- ½ tsp. fresh lemon juice
- 2 tsp. honey
- 1/8 tsp. ground cinnamon

Directions:
1. Coat each banana half with lemon juice.
2. Arrange the banana halves onto the greased "Sheet Pan" cut sides up.
3. Drizzle the banana halves with honey and sprinkle with cinnamon.
4. Press "Power Button" of Ninja Foodi Digital Air Fry Oven and turn the dial to select the "Air Fry" mode.
5. Press the Time button and again turn the dial to set the cooking time to 10 minutes.
6. Now push the Temp button and rotate the dial to set the temperature at 350 degrees F.
7. Press "Start/Pause" button to start.
8. When the unit beeps to show that it is preheated, open the lid.
9. Insert the "Sheet Pan" in oven.
10. Serve immediately.

Red Velvet Cupcakes

Servings: 12
Cooking Time: 12 Mins

Ingredients:
- For Cupcakes:
- 2 C. refined flour
- ¾ C. icing sugar
- 2 tsp. beet powder
- 1 tsp. cocoa powder
- ¾ C. peanut butter
- 3 eggs
- For Frosting:
- 1 C. butter
- 1 (8-ounce) package cream cheese, softened
- 2 tsp. vanilla extract
- ¼ tsp. salt
- 4½ C. powdered sugar
- For Garnishing:
- ½ C. fresh raspberries

Directions:
1. For cupcakes: in a bowl, add all the ingredients and with an electric whisker, whisk until well combined.
2. Place the mixture into silicone cups.
3. Press "Power Button" of Ninja Foodi Digital Air Fry Oven and turn the dial to select "Air Fry" mode.
4. Press "Time Button" and again turn the dial to set the cooking time to 12 minutes.
5. Now push "Temp Button" and rotate the dial to set the temperature at 340 degrees F.
6. Press "Start/Pause" button to start.
7. When the unit beeps to show that it is preheated, open the lid.
8. Arrange the silicone C. into the air fry basket and insert in the oven.
9. When cooking time is complete, open the lid and place the silicone C. onto a wire rack to cool for about 10 minutes.
10. Carefully invert the cupcakes onto the wire rack to completely cool before frosting.
11. For frosting: in a large bowl, mix well butter, cream cheese, vanilla extract, and salt.
12. Add the powdered sugar, one C. at a time, whisking well after each addition.
13. Spread frosting over each cupcake.
14. Garnish with raspberries and serve.

15. Serving Suggestions: Garnishing of sprinkles will add a festive touch in cupcakes.
16. Variation Tip: Measure the ingredients with care.

Chocolate Cake

Servings: 4
Cooking Time: 15 Mins

Ingredients:
- 3-1/2 tbsp. of butter, softened
- ¼ C. white sugar
- 1 tbsp. of apricot jam
- 1 egg
- 1 tbsp. cocoa powder, unsweetened
- 6 tbsp. of all-purpose flour

Directions:
1. Preheat your air fryer to 160 degrees C or 320 degrees F.
2. Apply cooking spray on a small tube pan.
3. Use an electric mixer to beat the butter and sugar together in your bowl. It should get creamy and light.
4. Add the jam and egg. Combine well by mixing.
5. Now sift in the cocoa powder, flour, and salt. Make sure to mix well.
6. Pour the batter into your pan. Take a spoon and with its backside, level the batter surface.
7. Transfer pan to your air fryer basket.
8. Cook for 10 minutes. A toothpick should come out clean from the cake's center.

Jalapeño Poppers

Servings: 6
Cooking Time: 13 Mins

Ingredients:

- 12 large jalapeño peppers
- 8 oz. cream cheese, softened
- ¼ C. scallion, chopped
- ¼ C. fresh cilantro, chopped
- ¼ tsp. onion powder
- ¼ tsp. garlic powder
- Salt, to taste
- 1/3 C. sharp cheddar cheese, grated

Directions:

1. Carefully cut off one-third of each pepper lengthwise and then scoop out the seeds and membranes.
2. In a bowl, mix together the cream cheese, scallion, cilantro, spices and salt.
3. Stuff each pepper with the cream cheese mixture and top with cheese.
4. Arrange the jalapeño peppers onto the greased sheet pan.
5. Press "Power Button" of Ninja Foodi Digital Air Fry Oven and turn the dial to select "Air Fry" mode.
6. Press "Time Button" and again turn the dial to set the cooking time to 13 minutes.
7. Now push "Temp Button" and rotate the dial to set the temperature at 400 degrees F.
8. Press "Start/Pause" button to start.
9. When the unit beeps to show that it is preheated, open the lid and insert the sheet pan in the oven.
10. When cooking time is complete, open the lid and transfer the jalapeño poppers onto a platter.
11. Serve immediately.
12. Serving Suggestions:
13. Variation Tip:

Spicy Spinach Chips

Servings: 4
Cooking Time: 10 Mins

Ingredients:

- 2 C. fresh spinach leaves, torn into bite-sized pieces
- ½ tbsp. coconut oil, melted
- 1/8 tsp. garlic powder
- Salt, as required

Directions:

1. In a large bowl and mix together all the ingredients.
2. Arrange the spinach pieces onto the greased "Sheet Pan".
3. Press "Power Button" of Ninja Foodi Digital Air Fry Oven and turn the dial to select the "Air Fry" mode.
4. Press the Time button and again turn the dial to set the cooking time to 10 minutes.
5. Now push the Temp button and rotate the dial to set the temperature at 300 degrees F.
6. Press "Start/Pause" button to start.
7. When the unit beeps to show that it is preheated, open the lid.
8. Insert the "Sheet Pan" in oven.
9. Toss the spinach chips once halfway through.

Fried Pickles

Servings: 8

Cooking Time: 10 Mins

Ingredients:

- 2 tbsp. of sriracha sauce
- ½ C. mayonnaise
- 1 egg
- ½ C. all-purpose flour
- 2 tbsp. of milk
- ¼ tsp. garlic powder
- 1 jar dill pickle chips

Directions:

1. Mix the sriracha sauce and mayonnaise together in a bowl.
2. Refrigerate until you can use it.
3. Heat your air fryer to 200 degrees C or 400 degrees F.
4. Drain the pickles. Use paper towels to dry them.
5. Now mix the milk and egg together in another bowl.
6. Also mix the cornmeal, flour, garlic powder, pepper, and salt in a third bowl.
7. Dip the pickle chips in your egg mix, and then in the flour mix. Coat both sides lightly. Press the mixture into chips lightly.
8. Apply cooking spray in the fryer basket.
9. Keep the chips in the fryer's basket.
10. Cook for 4 minutes. Flip over and cook for another 4 minutes.
11. Serve with the sriracha mayo.

Air-fried Butter Cake

Servings: 4
Cooking Time: 15 Mins

Ingredients:

- 1 egg
- 7 tbsp. of butter, room temperature
- 1-2/3 C. all-purpose flour
- ½ C. white sugar
- 6 tbsp. of milk

Directions:

1. Preheat your air fryer to 180 degrees C or 350 degrees F.
2. Apply cooking spray on a small tube pan.
3. Beat ¼ C. and 2 tbsp. of butter. It should be creamy and light.
4. Include the egg. Mix until it gets fluffy and smooth.
5. Stir in the salt and flour now.
6. Add milk. Mix the batter thoroughly.
7. Transfer the batter to your pan. Level the surface with a spoon's back.
8. Keep this pan in the basket of your air fryer.
9. Bake until you see a toothpick coming out clean when inserted.
10. Take out the cake. Set aside for cooling for 5 minutes.

Buffalo Chicken Wings

Servings: 5
Cooking Time: 16 Mins

Ingredients:

- 2 lb. frozen chicken wings, drums and flats separated
- 2 tbsp. olive oil
- 2-4 tbsp. Buffalo sauce
- ½ tsp. red pepper flakes, crushed
- Salt, to taste

Directions:

1. Coat the chicken wings with oil evenly.
2. Press "Power Button" of Ninja Foodi Digital Air Fry Oven and turn the dial to select "Air Fry" mode.
3. Press "Time Button" and again turn the dial to set the cooking time to 16 minutes.
4. Now push "Temp Button" and rotate the dial to set the temperature at 390 degrees F.
5. Press "Start/Pause" button to start.
6. When the unit beeps to show that it is preheated, open the lid.
7. Arrange the chicken wings into the air fry basket and insert in the oven.
8. After 7 minutes, flip the wings.
9. Meanwhile, in a large bowl, add the Buffalo sauce, red pepper flakes and salt and mix well.
10. When cooking time is complete, open the lid.
11. Transfer the wings into the bowl of Buffalo sauce and toss to coat well.
12. Serve immediately.
13. Serving Suggestions: Serving with blue cheese dip enhances the taste of these wings.
14. Variation Tip: To avoid spiciness, add a little sweetener in the sauce mixture.

Meat Recipes
Beef Kabobs

Servings: 4
Cooking Time: 10 Mins

Ingredients:
- 1 oz. beef ribs, cut into small 1-inch pieces
- 2 tbsp. soy sauce
- 1/3 C. low-fat sour cream
- 1 bell pepper
- ½ onion

Directions:
1. Mix soy sauce and sour cream in a bowl.
2. Keep the chunks of beef in the bowl. Marinate for 30 minutes' minimum.
3. Now cut the onion and bell pepper into one-inch pieces.
4. Soak 8 skewers in water.
5. Thread the bell pepper, onions, and beef on the skewers. Add some pepper.
6. Cook for 10 minutes in your pre-heated air fryer. Turn after 5 minutes.

Beef Sirloin Roast

Servings: 8
Cooking Time: 50 Mins

Ingredients:
- 1 tbsp. smoked paprika
- 1 tsp. ground cumin
- 1 tsp. garlic powder
- Salt and freshly ground black pepper, to taste
- 2½ lb. sirloin roast

Directions:
1. In a bowl, mix together the spices, salt and black pepper.
2. Rub the roast with spice mixture generously.
3. Place the sirloin roast into the greased baking pan.
4. Press "Power Button" of Ninja Foodi Digital Air Fry Oven and turn the dial to select "Air Roast" mode.
5. Press "Time Button" and again turn the dial to set the cooking time to 50 minutes.
6. Now push "Temp Button" and rotate the dial to set the temperature at 350 degrees F.
7. Press "Start/Pause" button to start.
8. When the unit beeps to show that it is preheated, open the lid and insert baking pan in the oven.
9. When cooking time is complete, open the lid and place the roast onto a platter for about 10 minutes before slicing.
10. With a sharp knife, cut the beef roast into desired sized slices and serve.
11. Serving Suggestions: Serve this roast with a topping of herbed butter.
12. Variation Tip: Rub the seasoning over the roast with your fingers, covering the entire exterior with an even layer.

Herbed Pork Chops

Servings: 3
Cooking Time: 12 Mins

Ingredients:

- 2 garlic cloves, minced
- ½ tbsp. fresh cilantro, chopped
- ½ tbsp. fresh rosemary, chopped
- ½ tbsp. fresh parsley, chopped
- 2 tbsp. olive oil
- ¾ tbsp. Dijon mustard
- 1 tbsp. ground coriander
- 1 tsp. sugar
- Salt, to taste
- 3 (6-ounce) (1-inch thick) pork chops

Directions:

1. In a bowl, mix together the garlic, herbs, oil, mustard, coriander, sugar, and salt.
2. Add the pork chops and coat with marinade generously.
3. Cover the bowl and refrigerate for about 2-3 hours.
4. Remove chops from the refrigerator and set aside at room temperature for about 30 minutes.
5. Press "Power Button" of Ninja Foodi Digital Air Fry Oven and turn the dial to select "Air Fry" mode.
6. Press "Time Button" and again turn the dial to set the cooking time to 12 minutes.
7. Now push "Temp Button" and rotate the dial to set the temperature at 390 degrees F.
8. Press "Start/Pause" button to start.
9. When the unit beeps to show that it is preheated, open the lid and grease the air fry basket.
10. Arrange chops into the prepared Air Fryer basket in a single layer and insert in the oven.
11. When cooking time is complete, open the lid and transfer the chops onto plates.
12. Serve hot.
13. Serving Suggestions: Serve thee chops with curried potato salad.
14. Variation Tip: Bring the pork chops to room temperature before cooking.

Glazed Lamb Chops

Servings: 4
Cooking Time: 15 Mins

Ingredients:

- 1 tbsp. Dijon mustard
- ½ tbsp. fresh lime juice
- 1 tsp. honey
- ½ tsp. olive oil
- Salt and freshly ground black pepper, to taste
- 4 (4-ounce) lamb loin chops

Directions:

1. In a black pepper large bowl, mix together the mustard, lemon juice, oil, honey, salt, and black pepper.
2. Add the chops and coat with the mixture generously.
3. Place the chops onto the greased sheet pan.
4. Press "Power Button" of Ninja Foodi Digital Air Fry Oven and turn the dial to select "Air Bake" mode.
5. Press "Time Button" and again turn the dial to set the cooking time to 15 minutes.
6. Now push "Temp Button" and rotate the dial to set the temperature at 390 degrees F.
7. Press "Start/Pause" button to start.
8. When the unit beeps to show that it is preheated, open the lid and insert the sheet pan in the oven.
9. Flip the chops once halfway through.
10. When cooking time is complete, open the lid and transfer the chops onto serving plates.
11. Serve hot.
12. Serving Suggestions: Serve the chops with mashed potatoes or polenta.
13. Variation Tip: Remember to pat dry the chops before seasoning.

Italian-style Meatballs

Servings: 12
Cooking Time: 35 Mins

Ingredients:
- 10 oz. lean beef, ground
- 3 garlic cloves, minced
- 5 oz. turkey sausage
- 2 tbsp. shallot, minced
- 1 large egg, lightly beaten
- 2 tbsp. of olive oil
- 1 tbsp. of rosemary and thyme, chopped

Directions:
1. Preheat your air fryer to 400 degrees F.
2. Heat oil and add the shallot. Cook for 1-2 minutes.
3. Add the garlic now and cook. Take out from the heat.
4. Add the garlic and cooked shallot along with the egg, turkey sausage, beef, rosemary, thyme, and salt. Combine well by stirring.
5. Shape the mixture gently into 1-1/2 inch small balls.
6. Keep the balls in your air fryer basket.
7. Cook your meatballs at 400 degrees F. They should turn light brown.
8. Take out. Keep warm.
9. Serve the meatballs over rice or pasta.

Braised Lamb Shanks

Servings: 4

Cooking Time: 2 Hours, 30 Mins

Ingredients:

- 4 lamb shanks
- 4 crushed garlic cloves
- 2 tbsp. of olive oil
- 3 C. of beef broth
- 2 tbsp. balsamic vinegar

Directions:

1. Rub pepper and salt on your lamb shanks. Keep in the baking pan.
2. Rub the smashed garlic on the lamb well.
3. Now cut the shanks with olive oil.
4. Keep underneath your lamb.
5. Keep the pan into the rack.
6. Roast for 20 minutes at 425 degrees F. Change to low for 2 hours at 250 F.
7. Add vinegar and 2 C. of broth.
8. Including the remaining broth after the 1st hour.

Lamb Sirloin Steak

Servings: 4
Cooking Time: 15 Mins

Ingredients:

- 1 oz. lamb sirloin steaks, boneless
- 5 garlic cloves
- 1 tsp. fennel, ground
- ½ onion
- 1 tsp. cinnamon, ground

Directions:

1. Add all the ingredients in your blender bowl other than the lamb chops.
2. Pulse and blend until you see the onion minced fine. All the ingredients should be blended well.
3. Now keep your lamb chops in a big-sized bowl.
4. Slash the meat and fat with a knife.
5. The marinade should penetrate.
6. Include the spice paste. Mix well.
7. Refrigerate the mixture for half an hour.
8. Keep the steaks of lamb in your air fryer basket.
9. Cook, flipping once.

Pork Meatloaf

Servings: 8
Cooking Time: 1 Hour 5 Mins

Ingredients:

- For Meatloaf:
- 2 lb. lean ground pork
- 1 C. quick-cooking oats
- ½ C. carrot, peeled and shredded
- 1 medium onion, chopped
- ½ C. fat-free milk
- ¼ of egg, beaten
- 2 tbsp. ketchup
- 1 tsp. garlic powder
- ¼ tsp. ground black pepper
- For Topping:
- ¼ C. ketchup
- ¼ C. quick-cooking oats

Directions:

1. For meatloaf: in a bowl, add all the ingredients and mix until well combined.
2. For topping: in another bowl, add all the ingredients and mix until well combined.
3. Transfer the mixture into a greased loaf pan and top with the topping mixture.
4. Press "Power Button" of Ninja Foodi Digital Air Fry Oven and turn the dial to select "Air Bake" mode.
5. Press "Time Button" and again turn the dial to set the cooking time to 65 minutes.
6. Now push "Temp Button" and rotate the dial to set the temperature at 350 degrees F.
7. Press "Start/Pause" button to start.
8. When the unit beeps to show that it is preheated, open the lid.
9. Arrange the loaf pan over the wire rack and insert in the oven.
10. When cooking time is complete, open the lid and place the loaf pan onto a wire rack for about 10 minutes.
11. Carefully invert the loaf onto the wire rack.
12. Cut into desired sized slices and serve.
13. Serving Suggestions: Baked cauliflower will nicely accompany this meatloaf.
14. Variation Tip: Add in a sprinkling of Italian seasoning in meatloaf.

Ranch Pork Chops

Servings: 4

Cooking Time: 15 Mins

Ingredients:

- 4 pork chops, boneless and center-cut
- 2 tsp. salad dressing mix

Directions:

1. Keep your pork chops on a plate.
2. Apply cooking spray on both sides lightly.
3. Sprinkle the seasoning mixture on both sides.
4. Allow to sit at room temperature for 5 minutes.
5. Apply cooking spray on the basket.
6. Preheat your air fryer to 200 degrees C or 390 degrees F.
7. Keep the chops in the air fryer. It shouldn't get overcrowded.
8. Cook for 5 minutes. Now flip your chops and cook for another 5 minutes.
9. Allow it to rest before serving.

Stuffed Pork Roll

Servings: 4
Cooking Time: 20 Mins

Ingredients:
- 1 scallion, chopped
- ¼ C. sun-dried tomatoes, chopped finely
- 2 tbsp. fresh parsley, chopped
- Salt and freshly ground black pepper, to taste
- 4 (6-ounce) pork cutlets, pounded slightly
- 2 tsp. paprika
- ½ tbsp. olive oil

Directions:
1. In a bowl, mix together the scallion, tomatoes, parsley, salt, and black pepper.
2. Spread the tomato mixture over each pork cutlet.
3. Roll each cutlet and secure with cocktail sticks.
4. Rub the outer part of rolls with paprika, salt and black pepper.
5. Coat the rolls with oil evenly.
6. Press "Power Button" of Ninja Foodi Digital Air Fry Oven and turn the dial to select "Air Fry" mode.
7. Press "Time Button" and again turn the dial to set the cooking time to 15 minutes.
8. Now push "Temp Button" and rotate the dial to set the temperature at 390 degrees F.
9. Press "Start/Pause" button to start.
10. When the unit beeps to show that it is preheated, open the lid and grease air fry basket.
11. Arrange pork rolls into the prepared air fry basket in a single layer and insert in the oven.
12. When cooking time is complete, open the lid and transfer the pork rolls onto serving plates.
13. Serve hot.
14. Serving Suggestions: Serve these pork rolls with creamed spinach.
15. Variation Tip: Drain the sun-dried tomatoes completely before using them.

Poultry Recipes

Herbed & Spiced Turkey Breast

Servings: 6
Cooking Time: 40 Mins

Ingredients:

- ¼ C. butter, softened
- 2 tbsp. fresh rosemary, chopped
- 2 tbsp. fresh thyme, chopped
- 2 tbsp. fresh sage, chopped
- 2 tbsp. fresh parsley, chopped
- Salt and ground black pepper, as required
- 1 (4-pound) bone-in, skin-on turkey breast
- 2 tbsp. olive oil

Directions:

1. In a bowl, add the butter, herbs, salt and black pepper and mix well.
2. Rub the herb mixture under skin evenly.
3. Coat the outside of turkey breast with oil.
4. Place the turkey breast into the greased baking pan.
5. Press "Power Button" of Ninja Foodi Digital Air Fry Oven and turn the dial to select the "Air Bake" mode.
6. Press the Time button and again turn the dial to set the cooking time to 40 minutes.
7. Now push the Temp button and rotate the dial to set the temperature at 350 degrees F.
8. Press "Start/Pause" button to start.
9. When the unit beeps to show that it is preheated, open the lid and insert baking pan in the oven.
10. Remove from oven and place the turkey breast onto a platter for about 5-10 minutes before slicing.
11. With a sharp knife, cut the turkey breast into desired sized slices and serve.

Herbed Chicken Drumsticks

Servings: 2
Cooking Time: 20 Mins

Ingredients:
- 1 tbsp. olive oil
- ½ tsp. dried thyme, crushed
- ½ tsp. dried rosemary, crushed
- ½ tsp. oregano, crushed
- Salt and freshly ground black pepper, to taste
- 2 (6-ounce) chicken drumsticks

Directions:
1. In a large bowl, place the oil, herbs, salt and black pepper and mix well.
2. Add the chicken drumsticks and coat with the mixture generously.
3. Place the chicken drumsticks into the greased baking pan.
4. Press "Power Button" of Ninja Foodi Digital Air Fry Oven and turn the dial to select "Air Fry" mode.
5. Press "Time Button" and again turn the dial to set the cooking time to 20 minutes.
6. Now push "Temp Button" and rotate the dial to set the temperature at 375 degrees F.
7. Press "Start/Pause" button to start.
8. When the unit beeps to show that it is preheated, open the lid and insert the baking pan in the oven.
9. When cooking time is complete, open the lid and transfer the chicken drumsticks onto serving plates.
10. Serve hot.
11. Serving Suggestions: Any kind of dipping sauce will be great for these drumsticks.
12. Variation Tip: You can use fresh herbs instead of dried herbs.

Blackened Chicken Breast

Servings: 2
Cooking Time: 20 Mins

Ingredients:
- 2 chicken breast halves, skinless and boneless
- 1 tsp. thyme, ground
- 2 tsp. of paprika
- 2 tsp. vegetable oil
- ½ tsp. onion powder

Directions:
1. Combine the thyme, paprika, onion powder, and salt together in your bowl.
2. Transfer the spice mix to a flat plate.
3. Rub vegetable oil on the chicken breast. Coat fully.
4. Roll the chicken pieces in the spice mixture. Press down, ensuring that all sides have the spice mix.
5. Keep aside for 5 minutes.
6. In the meantime, preheat your air fryer to 175 degrees C or 360 degrees F.
7. Keep the chicken in the air fryer basket. Cook for 8 minutes.
8. Flip once and cook for another 7 minutes.
9. Transfer the breasts to a serving plate. Serve after 5 minutes.

Seasoned Chicken Tenders

Servings: 2
Cooking Time: 10 Mins

Ingredients:
- 8 oz. chicken tenders
- 1 tsp. BBQ seasoning
- Salt and ground black pepper, as required

Directions:
1. Line the "Sheet Pan" with a lightly, greased piece of foil.
2. Set aside.
3. Season the chicken tenders with BBQ seasoning, salt and black pepper.
4. Arrange the chicken tenders onto the prepared "Sheet Pan" in a single layer.
5. Press "Power Button" of Ninja Foodi Digital Air Fry Oven and turn the dial to select the "Air Bake" mode.
6. Press the Time button and again turn the dial to set the cooking time to 10 minutes.
7. Now push the Temp button and rotate the dial to set the temperature at 450 degrees F.
8. Press "Start/Pause" button to start.
9. When the unit beeps to show that it is preheated, open the lid and insert "Sheet Pan" in the oven.
10. Serve hot.

Egg Frittata

Servings: 2

Cooking Time: 15 Mins

Ingredients:
- 4 eggs
- ¼ C. baby mushrooms, chopped
- ½ C. of milk
- 2 onions, chopped
- ¼ C. cheddar cheese

Directions:
1. Grease your pan with butter and keep it aside.
2. Whisk together the milk and eggs in a bowl. Blend well.
3. Stir in the mushrooms, onion, cheddar cheese, salt, and pepper. You can also include some hot sauce.
4. Now pour in the egg mix into your pan.
5. Transfer to your air fryer. Cook for 12 minutes at 360 degrees F.

Olive-brined Turkey Breast

Servings: 14
Cooking Time: 20 Mins

Ingredients:
- 3-1/2 oz. turkey breasts, boneless and skinless
- ½ C. buttermilk
- ¾ C. olive brine
- 2 sprigs of thyme
- 1 rosemary sprig

Directions:
1. Bring together the buttermilk and olive brine.
2. Keep the turkey breast in a plastic bag. Pour the buttermilk-brine mix into this.
3. Add the thyme sprigs and rosemary.
4. Seal and bag. Keep it refrigerated.
5. Take it out after 8 hours. Set it aside and wait for it to reach room temperature.
6. Preheat your air fryer to 175 degrees C or 350 degrees F.
7. Cook the turkey breast for 12 minutes.
8. Flip over and cook for another 5 minutes. The turkey's center shouldn't be pink.

Air Fryer Chicken Wings

Servings: 4
Cooking Time: 30 Mins

Ingredients:
- 1-1/2 oz. chicken wings
- 1 tsp. garlic powder
- 1 tsp. kosher salt
- 1 tbsp. of butter, unsalted and melted
- ½ C. hot sauce

Directions:
1. Keep your chicken wings in 1 layer. Use paper towels to pat them dry.
2. Sprinkle garlic powder and salt evenly.
3. Now keep these wings in your air fryer at 380°F.
4. Cook for 20 minutes. Toss after every 5 minutes. The wings should be cooked through and tender.
5. Bring up the temperature to 400 degrees F.
6. Cook for 5-8 minutes until it has turned golden brown and crispy.
7. Toss your wings with melted butter (optional) before serving.

Spiced Chicken Thighs

Servings: 4
Cooking Time: 20 Mins

Ingredients:
- 1 tsp. ground cumin
- 1 tsp. garlic powder
- ½ tsp. smoked paprika
- ½ tsp. ground coriander
- Salt and ground black pepper, as required
- 4 (5-ounce) chicken thighs

Directions:
1. In a large bowl, add the spices, salt and black pepper and mix well.
2. Coat the chicken thighs with oil and then rub with spice mixture.
3. Arrange the chicken thighs onto the sheet pan.
4. Press "Power Button" of Ninja Foodi Digital Air Fry Oven and turn the dial to select "Air Fry" mode.
5. Press "Time Button" and again turn the dial to set the cooking time to 20 minutes.
6. Now push "Temp Button" and rotate the dial to set the temperature at 400 degrees F.
7. Press "Start/Pause" button to start.
8. When the unit beeps to show that it is preheated, open the lid and insert the sheet pan in the oven.
9. Flip the chicken thighs once halfway through.
10. When cooking time is complete, open the lid and transfer the chicken thighs onto serving plates.
11. Serve hot.
12. Serving Suggestions: Serve with a fresh green salad.
13. Variation Tip: Adjust the ratio of spices according to your spice tolerance.

Nashville Chicken

Servings: 8
Cooking Time: 20 Mins

Ingredients:
- 2 oz. chicken breast, boneless
- 2 tbsp. hot sauce
- ½ C. of olive oil
- 3 large eggs
- 3 C. all-purpose flour
- 1 tsp. of chili powder
- 1-1/2 C. buttermilk

Directions:
1. Toss together the chicken, hot sauce, salt, and pepper in a bowl. Combine well.
2. Cover and refrigerate for three hours.
3. Pour flour into your bowl.
4. Now whisk the buttermilk and eggs together. Add 1 tbsp. of hot sauce.
5. For dredging your chicken, keep it in the flour first. Toss evenly for coating.
6. Keep it in your buttermilk mix. Then into the flour.
7. Keep them on your baking sheet.
8. Set the air fryer at 380 degrees. Place the tenders in your fryer.
9. Cook for 10 minutes.
10. For the sauce, whisk the spices and olive oil. Combine well.
11. Pour over the fried chicken immediately.

Roasted Cornish Game Hen

Servings: 4
Cooking Time: 16 Mins

Ingredients:
- ¼ C. olive oil
- 1 tsp. fresh rosemary, chopped
- 1 tsp. fresh thyme, chopped
- 1 tsp. fresh lemon zest, finely grated
- ¼ tsp. sugar
- ¼ tsp. red pepper flakes, crushed
- Salt and freshly ground black pepper, to taste
- 2 lb. Cornish game hen, backbone removed and halved

Directions:
1. In a bowl, mix together oil, herbs, lemon zest, sugar, and spices.
2. Add the hen portions and coat with the marinade generously.
3. Cover and refrigerate for about 24 hours.
4. In a strainer, place the hen portions and set aside to drain any liquid.
5. Press "Power Button" of Ninja Foodi Digital Air Fry Oven and turn the dial to select "Air Fry" mode.
6. Press "Time Button" and again turn the dial to set the cooking time to 16 minutes.
7. Now push "Temp Button" and rotate the dial to set the temperature at 390 degrees F.
8. Press "Start/Pause" button to start.
9. When the unit beeps to show that it is preheated, open the lid and grease the air fry basket.
10. Arrange the hen portions into the prepared basket and insert in the oven.
11. When cooking time is complete, open the lid and transfer the hen portions onto a platter.
12. Cut each portion in half and serve.
13. Serving Suggestions: Serve with dinner rolls.
14. Variation Tip: Place the hens in the basket, breast side up.

Asian Deviled Eggs

Servings: 12
Cooking Time: 15 Mins

Ingredients:
- 6 eggs
- 2 tbsp. of mayonnaise
- 1 tsp. soy sauce, low-sodium
- 1-1/2 tsp. of sesame oil
- 1 tsp. Dijon mustard

Directions:
1. Keep the eggs on the air fryer rack. Make sure that there is adequate space between them.
2. Set the temperature to 125 degrees C or 160 degrees F.
3. Air fry for 15 minutes.
4. Take out the eggs from your air fryer. Keep in an ice water bowl for 10 minutes.
5. Take them out of the water. Now peel and cut them in half.
6. Scoop out the yolks carefully. Keep in a food processor.
7. Add the sesame oil, mayonnaise, Dijon mustard, and soy sauce.
8. Process until everything combines well. The mixture should be creamy.
9. Fill up your piping bag with this yolk mixture. Distribute evenly into the egg whites. They should be heaping full.
10. You can garnish with green onions and sesame seeds (optional).

Crispy Roasted Chicken

Servings: 7
Cooking Time: 40 Mins

Ingredients:
- 1 (3½-pound) whole chicken, cut into 8 pieces
- Salt and ground black pepper, as required
- 2 C. buttermilk
- 2 C. all-purpose flour
- 1 tbsp. ground mustard
- 1 tbsp. garlic powder
- 1 tbsp. onion powder
- 1 tbsp. paprika

Directions:
1. Rub the chicken pieces with salt and black pepper.
2. In a large bowl, add the chicken pieces and buttermilk and refrigerate to marinate for at least 1 hour.
3. Meanwhile, in a large bowl, place the flour, mustard, spices, salt and black pepper and mix well.
4. Grease the cooking racks generously.
5. Remove the chicken pieces from bowl and drip off the excess buttermilk.
6. Coat the chicken pieces with the flour mixture, shaking any excess off.
7. Press "Power Button" of Ninja Foodi Digital Air Fry Oven and turn the dial to select the "Air Fry" mode.
8. Press the Time button and again turn the dial to set the cooking time to 20 minutes.
9. Now push the Temp button and rotate the dial to set the temperature at 390 degrees F.
10. Press "Start/Pause" button to start.
11. When the unit beeps to show that it is preheated, open the lid and grease "Air Fry Basket".
12. Arrange half of the chicken pieces into "Air Fry Basket" and insert in the oven.
13. Repeat with the remaining chicken pieces.
14. Serve immediately.

Turkish Chicken Kebab

Servings: 4
Cooking Time: 15 Mins

Ingredients:
- 1 oz. Chicken thighs, boneless and skinless
- ¼ C. Greek yogurt, plain
- 1 tbsp. tomato paste
- 1 tbsp. vegetable oil
- ½ tsp. cinnamon, ground

Directions:
1. Stir together the tomato paste, Greek yogurt, oil, cinnamon, salt, and pepper in a bowl. The spices should blend well into the yogurt.
2. Cut the chicken into 4 pieces.
3. Now include your chicken pieces into the mixture. Make sure that the chicken is coated well with the mixture.
4. Refrigerate for 30 minutes' minimum.
5. Take out chicken from your marinade.
6. Keep in your air fryer basket in a single layer.
7. Set your fryer to 370 degrees F. Cook the chicken pieces for 8 minutes.
8. Flip over and cook for another 4 minutes.

Bang-bang Chicken

Servings: 6
Cooking Time: 15 Mins

Ingredients:
- 1 oz. chicken breast tenderloins, small pieces
- ½ C. sweet chili sauce
- 1 C. of mayonnaise
- 1-1/2 C. bread crumbs
- 1/3 C. flour

Directions:
1. Whisk the sweet chili sauce and mayonnaise together in a bowl.
2. Spoon out 3 quarters of a C. from this. Set aside.
3. Keep flour in a plastic bag. Add the chicken and close this bag. Coat well by shaking.
4. Place the coated chicken in a large bowl with the mayonnaise mix.
5. Combine well by stirring.
6. Keep your bread crumbs in another plastic bag.
7. Place chicken pieces into the bread crumbs. Coat well.
8. Preheat your air fryer to 200 degrees C or 400 degrees F.
9. Transfer the chicken into the basket of your air fryer. Do not overcrowd.
10. Cook for 7 minutes.
11. Flip over and cook for another 4 minutes.
12. Transfer the chicken to a bowl. Pour over the reserved sauce.
13. You can also sprinkle some green onions before serving.

Peruvian Chicken Drumsticks & Green Crema

Servings: 6

Cooking Time: 15 Mins

Ingredients:
- 6 chicken drumsticks
- 2 garlic cloves, grated
- 1 tbsp. of olive oil
- 1 tbsp. honey
- 1 C. of baby spinach leaves, with stems removed
- ¼ C. cilantro leaves
- ¾ C. of sour cream

Directions:
1. Bring together the honey, garlic, pepper, and salt in a bowl.
2. Add the drumsticks. Coat well by tossing.
3. Keep the drumsticks in a vertical position in the basket. Keep them leaning against the wall of the basket.
4. Cook in your air fryer at 200 degrees C or 400 degrees F for 15 minutes.
5. In the meantime, combine the sour cream, cilantro leaves, pepper and salt in a food processor bowl.
6. Process until the crema has become smooth.
7. Drizzle the crema sauce over your drumsticks.

Fish & Seafood Recipes

Lemon Dill Mahi Mahi

Servings: 2
Cooking Time: 15 Mins

Ingredients:

- 2 fillets of Mahi Mahi, thawed
- 2 lemon slices
- 1 tbsp. olive oil
- 1 tbsp. lemon juice
- 1 tbsp. dill, chopped

Directions:

1. Combine the olive oil and lemon juice in a bowl. Stir.
2. Keep the fish fillets on a parchment paper sheet.
3. Brush the lemon juice mix on each side. Coat heavily.
4. Season with pepper and salt.
5. Add the chopped dill on top.
6. Keep the fillets of Mahi Mahi in your air fryer basket.
7. Cook at 400° F for 12 minutes.
8. Take out. Serve immediately.

Crumbed Fish

Servings: 4
Cooking Time: 12 Mins

Ingredients:
- 4 flounder fillets
- 1 C. bread crumbs
- 1 egg, beaten
- ¼ C. of vegetable oil
- 1 lemon, sliced

Directions:
1. Preheat your air fryer to 180 degrees C or 350 degrees F.
2. Mix the oil and bread crumbs in a bowl. Keep stirring until you see this mixture becoming crumbly and loose.
3. Now dip your fish fillets into the egg. Remove any excess.
4. Dip your fillets into the bread crumb mix. Make sure to coat evenly.
5. Keep the coated fillets in your preheated fryer gently.
6. Cook until you see the fish flaking easily with a fork.
7. Add lemon slices for garnishing.

Spiced Tilapia

Servings: 2
Cooking Time: 12 Mins

Ingredients:
- ¼ tsp. garlic powder
- ¼ tsp. onion powder
- ¼ tsp. ground cumin
- Salt and ground black pepper, as required
- 2 (6-ounce) tilapia fillets
- 1 tbsp. butter, melted

Directions:
1. In a small bowl, mix together the spices, salt and black pepper.
2. Coat the tilapia fillets with oil and then rub with spice mixture.
3. Press "Power Button" of Ninja Foodi Digital Air Fry Oven and turn the dial to select the "Air Fry" mode.
4. Press the Time button and again turn the dial to set the cooking time to 12 minutes.
5. Now push the Temp button and rotate the dial to set the temperature at 360 degrees F.
6. Press "Start/Pause" button to start.
7. When the unit beeps to show that it is preheated, open the lid.
8. Arrange the tilapia fillets over the greased "Wire Rack" and insert in the oven.
9. Flip the tilapia fillets once halfway through.
10. Serve hot.

Lemony Shrimp

Servings: 3
Cooking Time: 8 Mins

Ingredients:
- 2 tbsp. fresh lemon juice
- 1 tbsp. olive oil
- 1 tsp. lemon pepper
- ¼ tsp. paprika
- ¼ tsp. garlic powder
- 12 oz. medium shrimp, peeled and deveined

Directions:
1. In a large bowl, add all the ingredients except the shrimp and mix until well combined.
2. Add the shrimp and toss to coat well.
3. Arrange the shrimps onto a sheet pan.
4. Press "Power Button" of Ninja Foodi Digital Air Fry Oven and turn the dial to select "Air Fry" mode.
5. Press "Time Button" and again turn the dial to set the cooking time to 8 minutes.
6. Now push "Temp Button" and rotate the dial to set the temperature at 400 degrees F.
7. Press "Start/Pause" button to start.
8. When the unit beeps to show that it is preheated, open the lid and insert the sheet pan in the oven.
9. When cooking time is complete, open the lid and transfer the shrimp onto serving plates.
10. Serve hot.
11. Serving Suggestions: Serve with scalloped potatoes.
12. Variation Tip: Avoid shrimp that smell like ammonia.

Crusted Salmon

Servings: 2
Cooking Time: 15 Mins

Ingredients:
- 2 (6-ounce) skinless salmon fillets
- Salt and ground black pepper, as required
- 3 tbsp. walnuts, chopped finely
- 3 tbsp. quick-cooking oats, crushed
- 2 tbsp. olive oil

Directions:
1. Rub the salmon fillets with salt and black pepper evenly.
2. In a bowl, mix together the walnuts, oats and oil.
3. Arrange the salmon fillets onto the greased "Sheet Pan" in a single layer.
4. Place the oat mixture over salmon fillets and gently, press down.
5. Press "Power Button" of Ninja Foodi Digital Air Fry Oven and turn the dial to select the "Air Bake" mode.
6. Press the Time button and again turn the dial to set the cooking time to 15 minutes.
7. Now push the Temp button and rotate the dial to set the temperature at 400 degrees F.
8. Press "Start/Pause" button to start.
9. When the unit beeps to show that it is preheated, open the lid.
10. Insert the "Sheet Pan" in oven.
11. Serve hot.

Herbed Salmon

Servings: 2
Cooking Time: 10 Mins

Ingredients:
- 1 tbsp. fresh lime juice
- ½ tbsp. olive oil
- Salt and freshly ground black pepper, to taste
- 1 garlic clove, minced
- ½ tsp. fresh thyme leaves, chopped
- ½ tsp. fresh rosemary, chopped
- 2 (7-ounce) salmon fillets

Directions:
1. In a bowl, add all the ingredients except the salmon and mix well.
2. Add the salmon fillets and coat with the mixture generously.
3. Press "Power Button" of Ninja Foodi Digital Air Fry Oven and turn the dial to select "Air Bake" mode.
4. Press "Time Button" and again turn the dial to set the cooking time to 10 minutes.
5. Now push "Temp Button" and rotate the dial to set the temperature at 400 degrees F.
6. Press "Start/Pause" button to start.
7. When the unit beeps to show that it is preheated, open the lid.
8. Arrange the salmon fillets over the greased wire rack and insert in the oven.
9. Flip the fillets once halfway through.
10. When cooking time is complete, open the lid and transfer the salmon fillets onto serving plates.
11. Serve hot.
12. Serving Suggestions: Serve with steamed asparagus.
13. Variation Tip: For best result, use freshly squeezed lime juice.

Seasoned Catfish

Servings: 4
Cooking Time: 23 Mins

Ingredients:

- 4 (4-ounce) catfish fillets
- 2 tbsp. Italian seasoning
- Salt and freshly ground black pepper, to taste
- 1 tbsp. olive oil
- 1 tbsp. fresh parsley, chopped

Directions:

1. Rub the fish fillets with seasoning, salt and black pepper generously and then coat with oil.
2. Press "Power Button" of Ninja Foodi Digital Air Fry Oven and turn the dial to select "Air Fry" mode.
3. Press "Time Button" and again turn the dial to set the cooking time to 20 minutes.
4. Now push "Temp Button" and rotate the dial to set the temperature at 400 degrees F.
5. Press "Start/Pause" button to start.
6. When the unit beeps to show that it is preheated, open the lid and grease the air fry basket.
7. Arrange the fish fillets into the prepared air fry basket and insert in the oven.
8. Flip the fish fillets once halfway through.
9. When cooking time is complete, open the lid and transfer the fillets onto serving plates.
10. Serve hot with the garnishing of parsley.
11. Serving Suggestions: Quinoa salad will be a great choice for serving.
12. Variation Tip: Season the fish according to your choice.

Halibut & Shrimp with Pasta

Servings: 4
Cooking Time: 10 Mins

Ingredients:
- 14 oz. pasta
- 4 tbsp. pesto, divided
- 4 (4-ounce) halibut steaks
- 2 tbsp. olive oil
- ½ lb. tomatoes, chopped
- 8 large shrimp, peeled and deveined
- 2 tbsp. fresh lime juice
- 2 tbsp. fresh dill, chopped

Directions:
1. In the bottom of a baking pan, spread 1 tbsp. of pesto.
2. Place halibut steaks and tomatoes over pesto in a single layer and drizzle with the oil.
3. Now, place the shrimp on top in a single layer.
4. Drizzle with lime juice and sprinkle with dill.
5. Press "Power Button" of Ninja Foodi Digital Air Fry Oven and turn the dial to select "Air Fry" mode.
6. Press "Time Button" and again turn the dial to set the cooking time to 8 minutes.
7. Now push "Temp Button" and rotate the dial to set the temperature at 390 degrees F.
8. Press "Start/Pause" button to start.
9. When the unit beeps to show that it is preheated, open the lid.
10. Place the pan over the wire rack and insert in the oven.
11. Meanwhile, in a large pan of salted boiling water, add the pasta and cook for about 8-10 minutes or until desired doneness.
12. Drain the pasta and transfer into a large bowl.
13. Add the remaining pesto and toss to coat well.
14. When cooking time is complete, open the lid and divide the pasta onto serving plates.
15. Top with the fish mixture and serve immediately.
16. Serving Suggestions: Serve with the topping of freshly grated Parmesan.
17. Variation Tip: Linguine pasta will be the best choice for this recipe.

Crusted Sole

Servings: 2
Cooking Time: 15 Mins

Ingredients:
- 2 tsp. mayonnaise
- 1 tsp. fresh chives, minced
- 3 tbsp. Parmesan cheese, shredded
- 2 tbsp. panko breadcrumbs
- Salt and freshly ground black pepper, to taste
- 2 (4-ounce) sole fillets

Directions:
1. In a shallow dish, mix together the mayonnaise and chives.
2. In another shallow dish, mix together the cheese, breadcrumbs, salt and black pepper.
3. Coat the fish fillets with mayonnaise mixture and then roll in cheese mixture.
4. Arrange the sole fillets onto the greased sheet pan in a single layer.
5. Press "Power Button" of Ninja Foodi Digital Air Fry Oven and turn the dial to select "Air Bake" mode.
6. Press "Time Button" and again turn the dial to set the cooking time to 15 minutes.
7. Now push "Temp Button" and rotate the dial to set the temperature at 450 degrees F.
8. Press "Start/Pause" button to start.
9. When the unit beeps to show that it is preheated, open the lid and insert the sheet pan in the oven.
10. When cooking time is complete, open the lid and transfer the fish fillets onto serving plates.
11. Serve hot.
12. Serving Suggestions: Roasted potatoes make a great side for fish.
13. Variation Tip: If you want a gluten-free option then use pork rinds instead of breadcrumbs.

Glazed Salmon

Servings: 2
Cooking Time: 8 Mins

Ingredients:
- 2 (6-ounce) salmon fillets
- Salt, to taste
- 2 tbsp. honey

Directions:
1. Sprinkle the salmon fillets with salt and then coat with honey.
2. Press "Power Button" of Ninja Foodi Digital Air Fry Oven and turn the dial to select "Air Fry" mode.
3. Press "Time Button" and again turn the dial to set the cooking time to 8 minutes.
4. Now push "Temp Button" and rotate the dial to set the temperature at 355 degrees F.
5. Press "Start/Pause" button to start.
6. When the unit beeps to show that it is preheated, open the lid and grease the air fry basket.
7. Arrange the salmon fillets into the prepared air fry basket and insert in the oven.
8. When cooking time is complete, open the lid and transfer the salmon fillets onto serving plates.
9. Serve hot.
10. Serving Suggestions: Fresh baby greens will be great if served with glazed salmon.
11. Variation Tip: honey can be replaced with maple syrup too.

Vegetarian And Vegan Recipes

Glazed Mushrooms

Servings: 4
Cooking Time: 15 Mins

Ingredients:
- ¼ C. soy sauce
- ¼ C. honey
- ¼ C. balsamic vinegar
- 2 garlic cloves, chopped finely
- ½ tsp. red pepper flakes, crushed
- 18 oz. fresh Cremini mushrooms, halved

Directions:
1. In a bowl, place the soy sauce, honey, vinegar, garlic and red pepper flakes and mix well. Set aside.
2. Place the mushroom into the greased baking pan in a single layer.
3. Press "Power Button" of Ninja Foodi Digital Air Fry Oven and turn the dial to select "Air Bake" mode.
4. Press "Time Button" and again turn the dial to set the cooking time to 15 minutes.
5. Now push "Temp Button" and rotate the dial to set the temperature at 350 degrees F.
6. Press "Start/Pause" button to start.
7. When the unit beeps to show that it is preheated, open the lid.
8. Insert the baking pan in oven.
9. After 8 minutes of cooking, place the honey mixture in baking pan and toss to coat well.
10. When cooking time is complete, open the lid and transfer the mushrooms onto serving plates.
11. Serve hot.
12. Serving Suggestions: Topping of fresh chives or marjoram gives a delish touch to mushrooms.
13. Variation Tip: Maple syrup will be an excellent substitute for honey.

Tofu With Broccoli

Servings: 3
Cooking Time: 15 Mins

Ingredients:
- 8 oz. firm tofu, drained, pressed and cubed
- 1 head broccoli, cut into florets
- 1 tbsp. butter, melted
- 1 tsp. ground turmeric
- ¼ tsp. paprika
- Salt and ground black pepper, as required

Directions:
1. In a bowl, mix together all ingredients.
2. Place the tofu mixture in the greased cooking pan.
3. Press "Power Button" of Ninja Foodi Digital Air Fry Oven and turn the dial to select the "Air Fry" mode.
4. Press the Time button and again turn the dial to set the cooking time to 15 minutes.
5. Now push the Temp button and rotate the dial to set the temperature at 390 degrees F.
6. Press "Start/Pause" button to start.
7. When the unit beeps to show that it is preheated, open the lid.
8. Insert the baking pan in oven.
9. Toss the tofu mixture once halfway through.
10. Serve hot.

Fried Chickpeas

Servings: 4

Cooking Time: 20 Mins

Ingredients:
- 1 can chickpeas, rinsed and drained
- 1 tbsp. olive oil
- 1 tbsp. of nutritional yeast
- 1 tsp. garlic, granulated
- 1 tsp. of smoked paprika

Directions:
1. Spread the chickpeas on paper towels. Cover using a second paper towel later.
2. Allow them to dry for half an hour.
3. Preheat your air fryer to 180 degrees C or 355 degrees F.
4. Bring together the nutritional yeast, chickpeas, smoked paprika, olive oil, salt, and garlic in a mid-sized bowl. Coat well by tossing.
5. Now add your chickpeas to the fryer.
6. Cook for 16 minutes until they turn crispy. Shake them in 4-minute intervals.

Roasted Okra

Servings: 1

Cooking Time: 15 Mins

Ingredients:
- ½ oz. okra, trimmed ends and sliced pods
- ¼ tsp. salt
- 1 tsp. olive oil
- 1/8 tsp. black pepper, ground

Directions:
1. Preheat your air fryer to 175 degrees C or 350 degrees F.
2. Bring together the olive oil, okra, pepper, and salt in a mid-sized bowl.
3. Stir gently.
4. Keep in your air fryer basket. It should be in one single layer.
5. Cook for 5 minutes in the fryer. Toss once and cook for another 5 minutes.
6. Toss once more. Cook again for 2 minutes.

Roasted Vegetables

Servings: 4
Cooking Time: 20 Mins

Ingredients:
- 1 yellow squash, cut into small pieces
- 1 red bell pepper, seeded and cut into small pieces
- ¼ oz. mushrooms, cleaned and halved
- 1 tbsp. of extra-virgin olive oil
- 1 zucchini, cut into small pieces

Directions:
1. Preheat your air fryer. Keep the squash, red bell pepper, and mushrooms in a bowl.
2. Add the black pepper, salt, and olive oil. Combine well by tossing.
3. Keep the vegetables in your fryer basket.
4. Air fry them for 15 minutes. They should get roasted. Stir about halfway into the roasting time.

Potato-skin Wedges

Servings: 4
Cooking Time: 30 Mins

Ingredients:
- 4 medium potatoes
- 3 tbsp. of canola oil
- 1 C. of water
- ¼ tsp. black pepper, ground
- 1 tsp. paprika

Directions:
1. Keep the potatoes in a big-sized pot. Add salted water and keep covered. Boil.
2. Bring down the heat to medium. Let it simmer. It should become tender.
3. Drain the water on.
4. Keep in a bowl and place in the refrigerator until it becomes cool.
5. Bring together the paprika, oil, salt, and black pepper in a bowl.
6. Now cut the potatoes into small quarters. Toss them into your mixture.
7. Preheat your air fryer to 200 degrees C or 400 degrees F.
8. Add half of the wedges of potato into the fryer basket. Keep them skin-down. Don't overcrowd.
9. Cook for 15 minutes. It should become golden brown.

Broccoli With Cauliflower

Servings: 6
Cooking Time: 15 Mins

Ingredients:
- 1-pound broccoli, cut into 1-inch florets
- 1-pound cauliflower, cut into 1-inch florets
- 2 tbsp. butter
- Salt and ground black pepper, as required
- ¼ C. Parmesan cheese, grated

Directions:
1. In a pan of the boiling water, add the broccoli and cook for about 3-4 minutes.
2. Drain the broccoli well.
3. In a bowl, place the broccoli, cauliflower, oil, salt, and black pepper and toss to coat well.
4. Press "Power Button" of Ninja Foodi Digital Air Fry Oven and turn the dial to select the "Air Fry" mode.
5. Press the Time button and again turn the dial to set the cooking time to 15 minutes.
6. Now push the Temp button and rotate the dial to set the temperature at 400 degrees F.
7. Press "Start/Pause" button to start.
8. When the unit beeps to show that it is preheated, open the lid.
9. Arrange the veggie mixture in "Air Fry Basket" and insert in the oven.
10. Toss the veggie mixture once halfway through.
11. Remove from oven and transfer the veggie mixture into a large bowl.
12. Immediately, stir in the cheese and serve immediately.

Buttered Veggies

Servings: 3
Cooking Time: 20 Mins

Ingredients:
- 1 C. potatoes, chopped
- 1 C. beets, peeled and chopped
- 1 C. carrots, peeled and chopped
- 2 garlic cloves, minced
- Salt and ground black pepper, as required
- 3 tbsp. olive oil

Directions:
1. In a bowl, place all ingredients and toss to coat well.
2. Place the tofu mixture in the greased "Sheet Pan".
3. Press "Power Button" of Ninja Foodi Digital Air Fry Oven and turn the dial to select the "Air Bake" mode.
4. Press the Time button and again turn the dial to set the cooking time to 20 minutes.
5. Now push the Temp button and rotate the dial to set the temperature at 450 degrees F.
6. Press "Start/Pause" button to start.
7. When the unit beeps to show that it is preheated, open the lid.
8. Insert the "Sheet Pan" in oven.
9. Toss the veggie mixture once halfway through.
10. Serve hot.

Basil Tomatoes

Servings: 2
Cooking Time: 10 Mins

Ingredients:

- 3 tomatoes, halved
- Olive oil cooking spray
- Salt and freshly ground black pepper, to taste
- 1 tbsp. fresh basil, chopped

Directions:

1. Drizzle the cut sides of the tomato halves with cooking spray evenly.
2. Then, sprinkle with salt, black pepper and basil.
3. Press "Power Button" of Ninja Foodi Digital Air Fry Oven and turn the dial to select "Air Fry" mode.
4. Press "Time Button" and again turn the dial to set the cooking time to 10 minutes.
5. Now push "Temp Button" and rotate the dial to set the temperature at 320 degrees F.
6. Press "Start/Pause" button to start.
7. When the unit beeps to show that it is preheated, open the lid.
8. Arrange the tomatoes into the air fry basket and insert in the oven.
9. When cooking time is complete, open the lid and transfer the tomatoes onto serving plates.
10. Serve warm.
11. Serving Suggestions: You can use these tomatoes in pasta and pasta salads with a drizzle of balsamic vinegar.
12. Variation Tip: Fresh thyme can also be used instead of basil.

Sweet & Tangy Mushrooms

Servings: 4
Cooking Time: 15 Mins

Ingredients:
- ¼ C. soy sauce
- ¼ C. honey
- ¼ C. balsamic vinegar
- 2 garlic cloves, chopped finely
- ½ tsp. red pepper flakes, crushed
- 18 oz. cremini mushrooms, halved

Directions:
1. In a bowl, place the soy sauce, honey, vinegar, garlic and red pepper flakes and mix well. Set aside.
2. Place the mushroom into the greased baking pan in a single layer.
3. Press "Power Button" of Ninja Foodi Digital Air Fry Oven and turn the dial to select the "Air Bake" mode.
4. Press the Time button and again turn the dial to set the cooking time to 15 minutes.
5. Now push the Temp button and rotate the dial to set the temperature at 350 degrees F.
6. Press "Start/Pause" button to start.
7. When the unit beeps to show that it is preheated, open the lid.
8. Insert the baking pan in oven.
9. After 8 minutes of cooking, place the honey mixture in baking pan and toss to coat well.
10. Serve hot.

Potato Gratin

Servings: 4
Cooking Time: 20 Mins

Ingredients:

- 2 large potatoes, sliced thinly
- 5½ tbsp. cream
- 2 eggs
- 1 tbsp. plain flour
- ½ C. cheddar cheese, grated

Directions:

1. Press "Power Button" of Ninja Foodi Digital Air Fry Oven and turn the dial to select "Air Fry" mode.
2. Press "Time Button" and again turn the dial to set the cooking time to 10 minutes.
3. Now push "Temp Button" and rotate the dial to set the temperature at 355 degrees F.
4. Press "Start/Pause" button to start.
5. When the unit beeps to show that it is preheated, open the lid.
6. Arrange the potato slices in the air fry basket and insert in the oven.
7. Meanwhile, in a bowl, add cream, eggs and flour and mix until a thick sauce forms.
8. When cooking time is complete, open the lid and remove the potato slices from the basket.
9. Divide the potato slices in 4 ramekins evenly and top with the egg mixture evenly, followed by the cheese.
10. Press "Power Button" of Ninja Foodi Digital Air Fry Oven and turn the dial to select "Air Fry" mode.
11. Press "Time Button" and again turn the dial to set the cooking time to 10 minutes.
12. Now push "Temp Button" and rotate the dial to set the temperature at 390 degrees F.
13. Arrange the ramekins in the air fry basket and insert in the oven.
14. Press "Start/Pause" button to start.
15. When cooking time is complete, open the lid and remove the ramekins from the oven.
16. Serve warm.
17. Serving Suggestions: Serve this gratin with fresh lettuce.
18. Variation Tip: Make sure to cut the potato slices thinly.

Cheesy Kale

Servings: 3
Cooking Time: 15 Mins

Ingredients:
- 1-pound fresh kale, tough ribs removed and chopped
- 3 tbsp. olive oil
- Salt and ground black pepper, as required
- 1 C. goat cheese, crumbled
- 1 tsp. fresh lemon juice

Directions:
1. In a bowl, add the kale, oil, salt and black pepper and mix well.
2. Press "Power Button" of Ninja Foodi Digital Air Fry Oven and turn the dial to select the "Air Fry" mode.
3. Press the Time button and again turn the dial to set the cooking time to 15 minutes.
4. Now push the Temp button and rotate the dial to set the temperature at 340 degrees F.
5. Press "Start/Pause" button to start.
6. When the unit beeps to show that it is preheated, open the lid and grease "Air Fry Basket".
7. Arrange the kale into "Air Fry Basket" and insert in the oven.
8. Remove from oven and immediately, transfer the kale mixture into a bowl.
9. Stir in the cheese and lemon juice and serve hot.

Parmesan Asparagus

Servings: 3
Cooking Time: 10 Mins

Ingredients:

- 1 lb. fresh asparagus, trimmed
- 1 tbsp. Parmesan cheese, grated
- 1 tbsp. butter, melted
- 1 tsp. garlic powder
- Salt and freshly ground black pepper, to taste

Directions:

1. In a bowl, mix together the asparagus, cheese, butter, garlic powder, salt, and black pepper.
2. Press "Power Button" of Ninja Foodi Digital Air Fry Oven and turn the dial to select "Air Fry" mode.
3. Press "Time Button" and again turn the dial to set the cooking time to 10 minutes.
4. Now push "Temp Button" and rotate the dial to set the temperature at 400 degrees F.
5. Press "Start/Pause" button to start.
6. When the unit beeps to show that it is preheated, open the lid and grease the air fry basket.
7. Arrange the veggie mixture into the prepared air fry basket and insert in the oven.
8. When cooking time is complete, open the lid and transfer the asparagus onto serving plates.
9. Serve hot.
10. Serving Suggestions: Serve with the garnishing of pine nuts.
11. Variation Tip: you can use fresh garlic instead of garlic powder.

Green Beans & Mushroom Casserole

Servings: 6
Cooking Time: 12 Mins

Ingredients:

- 24 oz. fresh green beans, trimmed
- 2 C. fresh button mushrooms, sliced
- 3 tbsp. olive oil
- 2 tbsp. fresh lemon juice
- 1 tsp. ground sage
- 1 tsp. garlic powder
- 1 tsp. onion powder
- Salt and freshly ground black pepper, to taste
- 1/3 C. French fried onions

Directions:

1. In a bowl, add the green beans, mushrooms, oil, lemon juice, sage, and spices and toss to coat well.
2. Press "Power Button" of Ninja Foodi Digital Air Fry Oven and turn the dial to select "Air Fry" mode.
3. Press "Time Button" and again turn the dial to set the cooking time to 12 minutes.
4. Now push "Temp Button" and rotate the dial to set the temperature at 400 degrees F.
5. Press "Start/Pause" button to start.
6. When the unit beeps to show that it is preheated, open the lid and grease the air fry basket.
7. Arrange the mushroom mixture into the prepared air fry basket and insert in the oven.
8. Shake the mushroom mixture occasionally.
9. When cooking time is complete, open the lid and transfer the mushroom mixture into a serving dish.
10. Top with fried onions and serve.
11. Serving Suggestions: Fresh salad will accompany this casserole nicely.
12. Variation Tip: Any kind of fresh mushrooms can be used.

Spicy Potato

Servings: 4
Cooking Time: 25 Mins

Ingredients:
- 2 C. water
- 6 russet potatoes, peeled and cubed
- ½ tbsp. extra-virgin olive oil
- ½ of onion, chopped
- 1 tbsp. fresh rosemary, chopped
- 1 garlic clove, minced
- 1 jalapeño pepper, chopped
- ½ tsp. garam masala powder
- ¼ tsp. ground cumin
- ¼ tsp. red chili powder
- Salt and ground black pepper, as required

Directions:
1. In a large bowl, add the water and potatoes and set aside for about 30 minutes.
2. Drain well and pat dry with the paper towels.
3. In a bowl, add the potatoes and oil and toss to coat well.
4. Press "Power Button" of Ninja Foodi Digital Air Fry Oven and turn the dial to select the "Air Fry" mode.
5. Press the Time button and again turn the dial to set the cooking time to 5 minutes.
6. Now push the Temp button and rotate the dial to set the temperature at 330 degrees F.
7. Press "Start/Pause" button to start.
8. When the unit beeps to show that it is preheated, open the lid.
9. Arrange the potato cubes in "Air Fry Basket" and insert in the oven.
10. Remove from oven and transfer the potatoes into a bowl.
11. Add the remaining ingredients and toss to coat well.
12. Press "Power Button" of Ninja Foodi Digital Air Fry Oven and turn the dial to select the "Air Fry" mode.
13. Press the Time button and again turn the dial to set the cooking time to 20 minutes.
14. Now push the Temp button and rotate the dial to set the temperature at 390 degrees F.
15. Press "Start/Pause" button to start.
16. When the unit beeps to show that it is preheated, open the lid.
17. Arrange the potato mixture in "Air Fry Basket" and insert in the oven.
18. Serve hot.

Printed in Great Britain
by Amazon

80323966R00047